AF248777

Also by D.C. Maplesden (with Joan Maplesden)

Deadly Design

From the
Bruce Hamilton Series:

Trojan Steers
Surrogape
Creatures of Hammock

Enchanted

(In the Land of Enchantment)

And Other Poems

Enchanted

(In the Land of Enchantment)

And Other Poems

D. C. Maplesden

Lomaland Books, Inc.
Lamy, New Mexico

Enchanted
(In the Land of Enchantment)

And Other Poems

Copyright © by
LomaLand Books, Inc.

LomaLand Books, Inc.
33 Willa Cather Road
Lamy, New Mexico 87540

Printed in the U.S.A. All rights reserved
Library of Congress Control Number: 2002092664
ISBN 1-930371-05-5

First Edition
2002
10 9 8 7 6 5 4 3 2 1

Contents

ANIMALS

PEOPLE

MISCELLANEOUS

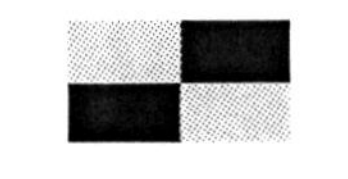

ANIMALS

Ashlings Strengths

Only one year old and very tall,
As high as the table in the hall.

Not the biggest, or the most might,
But none are close to her in height.

One of ten, eight brothers and a sister,
Ashling the aggressive one of the litter.

When we walked in the run to pick a pup,
Ashling nudged her siblings away, came right up.

Each day of her life she eats a pound,
Of balanced dog food, then dashes around.

At fourteen months, still a pup, loves to play.
If you have the time, she'll run all day.

Powerful white teeth, never used to bite,
She loves to have them polished bright.

Dogs are used in packs to run,
Ashling strives for number one.

She nibbles on anything coming her way,
Tennis balls or rawhide shredded in a day.

A hard nylon bone the only recourse,
Or maybe a big bone from a horse.

Big dogs must be taught to obey,
They need training every day.

First to heel, daily you train,
To get the message to her brain.

Soon she learns not to lead,
But walk beside, commanded to heed.

To sit whenever the master stops,
Of course, at first, she merely flops.

But soon she stately and silently sits,
No more terrible tantrum fits.

Next comes the order, "Ashling, stay."
Even when mistress walks away.

Then comes another command,
To come with a motion of the hand.

You see she's learning to be polite,
She's getting good manners just right.

Ashling is learning to guard the house,
Keeping out predators, even a mouse.

Other dogs look at Ashling's size,
Decide to take off over the rise.

She seldom whines or makes a noise,
But likes to race 'round with her toys.

When she grows older she'll be more quiet,
And eat a healthful senior diet.
She eats great food to make her strong,
Like good boys and girls, she won't do wrong.

Given a wash with warm water she's hosed,
Doesn't worry if her eyes are closed.
She's given a bath with "no-tears" shampoo,
The kind that kids wash with too.

Many things cause eyes bad stings,
But "no-tears" shampoo isn't one of those things.
She likes always to be neat and clean,
When dry and brushed has a pretty sheen.

On a hike in the mountains she spots a snake,
Not one that harms, but no chances to take,
She stops and gives out a rare bark.
Her mistress says, "What's this lark?
If she's making a noise there's something wrong,
She never whines or makes a song."
So all stop short and then they see,
A friendly snake beside a tree.
"Good girl," they say, "to be alert."
It's a good snake, but round it we skirt.

She told us to always be careful,
The only way she knows, to give us an earful.
With seldom used vocal chords,
She's given us the equivalent of words.

If horses along the back trail ride,
She puts her feet up on the wall, doesn't hide,
But is telling the horses to stay clear,
Although it's plain they've nothing to fear.
The riders, seeing Ashling on guard,
Pull on the reins, turn around hard.

Don't think of big dogs to be scared,
Ashling is gentle and not to be feared.
To protect, she is always ready,
Her friendship is steady .
One's best friend, she's very loyal,
Sits beside you looking Royal.

She seldom growls, has a withering glance,
She's quiet but has an imposing stance.
Ashling's Message: No need to go to angry lengths,
Just rely on your inner strengths.

FADD (Feline Attention Deficit Disorder)

FADD, is not merely a passing fad,
It appears to be permanent in our lad.
Andy (Contrariwise Cat, C.C., L.E. Katz) I mean,
He's carrying this fault in a gene.

"Pile up my food in a heaping mound,"
He takes two bites, starts peering around.
Begins racing about, displaces a rug,
Uses the litter box, comes out looking smug.

Andy goes to the toy bag, finds a red pepper,
Not really a hot one, this one has a zipper.
Inside it is loaded with potent catnip.
Andy nibbles a moment, then goes on a trip,
To feline heaven, where, spaced out he dreams,
Of ambushing mice and other wild schemes.

The men outside are building a wall,
Andy supervises, so it won't fall.

Basically not a lap cat, "No fussing, please.
Don't try that grooming, I ain't got fleas."

He checks every nook and cranny in the house,
"O.K., it's all right, there's nary a mouse."

Several times a day, "I'll have a wee sleep.
Got to get my rest, all else can keep."

Mister Katz, he whined to me,
"I can't even climb a tree.
Because, (sigh), I have no claws.
I've really useless, bare front paws."

Andy obviously can't catch rats,
Why? As he said his paws have no claws.
But he chews on mats, and baby dolls,
Climbs on rocks with his tender paws.

Mr. Andy had a past misuse,
He was subject to "cat abuse."
But ever so slowly he's come around.
When petted, emits a deep purring sound.

Andy several times daily has a rite,
Lies down on his back, passers-by get a bite.
He s-t-r-e-t-c-h-e-s full-length on the floor,
Fills narrow ways. "Kitty bars the door."

It's All Bull

The Judge felt Rex's right, then left horn.
It came off in his hand, Joe shrugged his shoulders.
The horn had been knocked off on unloading,
And hastily shoved onto the stub, to get by in the ring.
The Judge ran his hand down the back and loin,
Easily detected the cut "tie" on the backbone.
The loin flushed out with olive oil.
He said nothing, felt down the back to the tail,
The end of which, lightly glued on, fell to the ground.
The switch had been wrenched off in the truck gate.
The Judge gave Joe a sly grin, reached for the testicles.
"At least they're real, said Joe, "He's all bull."

Down the line all bulls had testicles, horns and tails,
And they too had cosmetic surgery along the back and loin.
The Judge conferred to Rex the Blue Ribbon,
With relative ease and clear conscience.

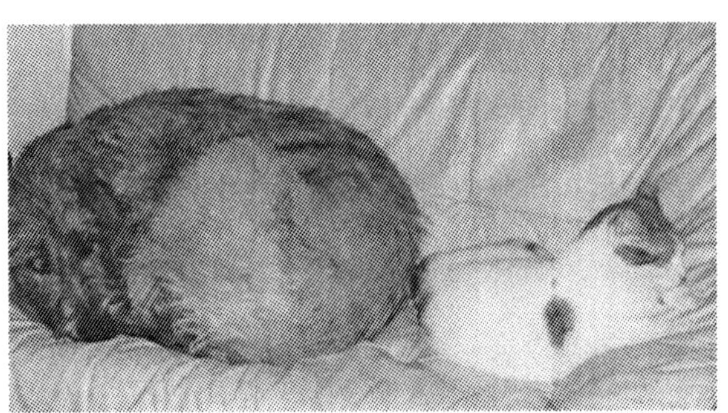

Jealousy

"Andy, you got a crouton, I didn't."
Or "You had an extra pat on the head."
Should Ashling be acting this way to Andy?
Why does Andy do likewise to Ashling?

Andy, Alley Cat, rescued from abuse.
Orange and white ringed periscope tail.
Ashling, Irish Wolfhound, in alpha mode,
Ears flopped up, brindle coat askew.

People of anthropomorphism accused,
But perhaps it should be so.
Dogs and cats domesticated for ten thousand years,
Still not given the credit deserved.

Now when pigs, ferrets, snakes, other species,
Fill our lives with emotions and reactions,
We begin to realize what motivates dogs and cats.
They share feelings and thoughts with humans.

Pets and people possess similar attributes,
Having evolved from a common base.
The jealousy exhibited by Andy and Ashling,
Is a reflection of a human trait.

Pack Animals

One hundred thousand years ago, man domesticated wolves.
By selective breeding they have produced,
Present breeds of dogs, Chihuahua to Irish Wolfhound.
A little, perhaps a lot, of anthropomorphism has crept in,
Dogs names and characteristics are described in human terms.

But wait.
Reverse teaching has gone on.

Dogs by nature are pack animals,
Now they've trained *Homo sapiens*.
People have become "pack animals."

Congregated in a sports arena, huddling together,
They're led in a "Wave" by costumed mascots, pseudo-animals.
On the Interstate, cars and trucks, regardless of the route,
Travel in packs, twenty feet apart—at eighty miles an hour.
Eat most meals in crowded restaurants, drink in bars.
Shop for everything in malls or massive supermarkets.
Hundreds of thousands jam together at rock concerts.
No one wants to be alone.

Why do dogs travel in packs?
Probably for hunting and protection.
Why do humans socialize in packs?
Are there reasons other than being taught by canines?

Purebred Proof

Want to buy a purebred bitch,
Ever think there may be a hitch?
Purebreds less pure than they seem,
Because breeders have a nefarious scheme?

They have put in a zinger,
And you've bought a ringer?
No one around to observe a mating,
The sire is one with a lower rating.

For some time there have been scams,
In any enterprise there are flim flams.
But now it's hoped with tests of DNA,
That such bad blood will be driven away.

The American Kennel Club found in a test,
Ninety-percent were O.K., not so the rest.

What to do if you're to be sure,
That your new pup is genetically pure?
Before you go forth insist on a test,
Improves the odds you'll get the best.

The Contrariwise Cat

The Contrariwise Cat won't do that or this,
But he'll do this or that, with comparative bliss.

When you put in fresh litter, he throws it around,
Meaning, "Take me outside, I must use the ground."

With any small lamp, this Contrariwise rake,
Will play Don Quixote, until they all break.

A challenge to bite, an electrical wire,
He won't be happy until it's on fire.

"Don't walk on the counter with cat littered feet."
Is to him an invite to make it his beat.

If you offer a pear, he wants a banana,
Don't try to encumbrance him with a bandanna.

When a streak of lightning flies through the house,
It isn't a comet, C.C.'s chasing a mouse.

That undulating globule under the mat,
Is not alien bodies, it's Contrariwise Cat.

Ashes left in the fireplace are stirred with panache,
Dons four black booties and a giant mustache.

Mr. Katz was too fat, tried to reduce,
Was fretting from a burden of "cat abuse."

With love and care he slowly came 'round,
Likes to be petted, makes a deep purring sound.

The Contrariwise Cat Turns Three

Andy Star, the Contrariwise Cat, at three,
Has acquired a degree of maturity.
No breaking lamps, chewing on wires,
Occasionally treads the ashes from fires.

At breakfast time he's on a chair,
Next to Joan, then nips her ear.
To let her know he wants a taste,
"Don't let that milk go to waste."

Keeps on pushing to raise the shade,
So he can view birds in the glade.
He likes to sniff the clean, fresh air,
When his back arches, he's spied a hare.

When bedtime looms he's in your face,
Herded to the bathroom, but at his own pace.
Mr. Katz walks very slowly ahead,
While he leads you to his nice warm bed.

When Andy was young no way could you cuddle,
An errant cat, now he likes to huddle.
When in bed or at your desk sitting,
He comes up and wants some petting.

Andy's friend, Ashling, Irish Wolfhound,
Really doesn't like Andy around.
So often you'll see them face to face,
But Andy's not easy to put into place.

All in all, Andy became a great cat.
Everyone agrees he's overly fat,
But he's overcome most aggressive traits,
At least the ones that everyone hates.

With kids, parents are a distant third,
It's genes and peers mold a prize or a nerd.
But Andy has evolved from brat to good cat,
Having good owners orchestrated all that.

The Other Half

I told you of Andy, the Contrariwise Cat.
Now there's Ashling, Irish Wolfhound brat.
Have you ever slept peacefully in your bed,
When plops on you, a thirty-pound head?
Annealed nylon bone, held like a cigar,
To be hit by a rock would be better by far.
A flowing beard drips with ice-water too.
Just two animals, but seems like a zoo.
On the telephone, hammering sounds are the bone,
Being dropped on the tile throughout the home.
Will she soon behave better, forget the strife?
She'd better, the breed has a very short life.

PEOPLE

A Birthday Wish

May your day begin with bright corpuscles
in the Sangre de Cristo sunrise.
May smiling down at you be the happy face
of Old Baldy.
May your day be capped with a Georgia O'Keeffe
sunset over the Jemez.
May the day bring much happiness
from those who love you
May your coming year be the best ever
you could imagine.
In other words, may you have a
sensational Santa Fe Day and Year.

A Kindred Soul

What happens to a good soul when life is snuffed?
Parts go to those of kindred strengths.
So now that Diana's is dispersed,
Surely you feel enhanced psyche.
The good people do lives long after them.
Although you're not half along,
You've given much with more to come.

A QLA Day in Rhyme
(Quality Life Assured)

Breakfast

A cup of coffee, you're on your way.
Is this your breakfast every day?
You've burned up protein through the night,
Need a balanced meal to nurture cells right.

Breakfast, the most important meal,
To ensure a healthy, vibrant feel.
In mid-morning you won't have to snack,
On high fat and calories, a habit to crack.

"What is a good breakfast?" you might say,
"One I can eat most every day,
And not get tired of the same old fare.
Then embrace obesity and not care."

A good menu for most days,
Is one served in several ways.
But basically the following food,
Eat it and share a positive mood.

A multi-vitamin-mineral tablet,
Always a very good habit.
Our soils have become depleted,
But poor nutrition can be defeated.

Orange juice for fluid, vitamin C,
Other natural juices are good for thee.
Cereal for protein, fiber and energy,
Together with milk, rendered fat free.

Some fruit to add antioxidants galore,
Use the one that you crave for.
Except to remember, it's a fact,
Avocados, cholesterol free, with fat are packed.

A non-caloric beverage of your choice,
Add up the calories and rejoice.
You've had a breakfast that's complete,
Your body with nutrients is replete.

Lunch

Lunch, a conundrum because the dish,
With fat, calories and salt, is what you wish.
Don't go for a salad, mostly greens,
The result is not what it seems.

Adding a no-fat dressing won't do the trick.
The combination won't make you sick,
But it's deficient in nutrients, so you see,
You'll be hungry and pig-out about three.

Soup, bread and cheese would serve the bill.
Or a low fat sandwich gives you fill.
And don't forget what beverages do,
Give hidden calories, not one or two.

Water is best, but you may grow tired,
Lemonade or iced tea may get you up-fired.
If you wish, add synthetic sweets,
Low calorie and add luster to many eats.

Dinner

From four o'clock, a whole different game,
You're hungry and thirsty, what's to blame?
It's the hormonal low point of your day,
So before dinner, carefully wend your way.

Count every calorie you drink or eat,
It's really not a difficult feat.
Per gram, fat has nine calories, sugars four,
And alcohol seven, per gram, three more.

For dinner a salad is fine and filling,
Fix up a mixed one if you're willing,
Several veggies to cut and chop.
Easy on the oil you sprinkle on top.

Eat mostly veggies with your meat or fish,
Three to four ounces of entree comprise a dish.
Pasta is great, filling, good taste.
Mexican dishes can be prepared in haste.

Go easy on desserts with high fat,
Cakes, cookies and pies often that.
But some low fat treats are high caloric too,
So the choice is really up to you.

In Conclusion

In your menus don't merely calculate fat,
Balanced nutrition is more than that.
You can count fat grams, perhaps a pain,
But if calories are ignored, fat you'll gain.

A Scientific Look at Love

Are human feelings physics or chemistry?
Biochemistry reactions are electron driven,
Thus all human functions,
Are electricity, a part of physics.

Love is an electrical charge.
Compare one's electron flow to three-way bulbs,
Which come in different wattages,
Twenty-five, fifty and a hundred, or higher.

First sight may turn on maximum wattage,
That may be sustained indefinitely,
But more likely cannot without arcing,
Flashing brightly, burning out.

A low wattage that gradually increases,
May or may not reach the built in maximum.
May fade into oblivion,
Or be sustained from low to high.

Beginnings at one range or another,
May oscillate greatly or mildly, up or down.
Ideally in a middle, balanced range,
Hoping for high power bursts.

Relating hormone levels to sexual electricity,
There is a bell curve for both sexes.
Those with a ratio high in testosterone,
Those with a ratio high in estrogen.

The outliers of male or female,
High levels of testosterone, grossly male,
High levels of estrogen, petitely female,
Share reduced sexual power, lower drive.

We're all driven by different levels of electricity.
Compare your output levels to a three-way bulb.
Make the best use possible of your electron potential.
Aim for balance, but hope for peaks of pleasure.

Advice

People accept many aphorisms without thought,
But some, perhaps all, should be questioned.

George Bernard Shaw wrote,
"He who can, does, He who cannot teaches."
Obviously many holes in this.

It has been stated that, "Experience is the best teacher,
But demands the highest salary."
The costs may not all be monetary.

The French say: "No frigid women, only clumsy men."
I asked a guru, who replied
"Not true or relevant."

"What's a man to do," I asked.
"Keep beard, finger and toenails short,
Be sweet smelling, your kisses soft."

Amy

Amy, a star shining bright,
A beacon cutting a misty night.
She is the center, people defer,
To the startling regality of her.
At her bridal shower, so it will be,
At her wedding, Juliet in reality.

Bitter Ex At The Wedding

Her butterfly tattooed left breast,
Flopped out of a diaphanous, flowered dress.
Body thin, hair dark ochre and frizzled,
Flipped as she danced; sexuality sizzled.
A scorned divorcee, she wouldn't let go,
At her son's wedding she put on a show.

Her ex-spouse was there, he'd caused the rift.
Married the pregnant, baby-sitter teen; ex miffed.
A dapper physician, sedate, out to please.
Promiscuous, litigious ex-wife, exuding sleaze,
Egotistical stories with great fervor we hear,
With more holes than Swiss cheese can bear.

Don't Trust The Experts

Should you trust the experts, of which I'm one?
The answer is no, your works not done,
Until you've thought through any case,
Exploring the situation thoroughly, without haste.

Don't accept one person's opinion—never, never,
Rely on your own judgment, forever and ever.
And it's not just in medicine and health,
Or in financial dealings to increase your wealth.

Are your accountants and financial advisors billionaires?
Can MD's diagnose in 23 seconds, even though millionaires?
Not now, but later computers will add a lot,
Giving quick insight to what you've got.

Feed your common sense into every endeavor,
Challenge every opinion no matter whatever.
To the "expert" you may cause disturbance and strife,
But it's your money, your future, your very life.

Fame, Notoriety and Hero

"In the future everyone will be world-famous for fifteen minutes,"
Andy Warhol

The lines between fame, notoriety and hero
Are becoming hopelessly blurred.

Fortunately "sport" is often added as a modifier of "hero,"
It describes a lesser hero,
Merely designating physical prowess.

The saddest part is that
The distorted meanings of these three words,
Used indiscriminately by poorly educated journalists,
Become accepted.

A further decline and fall
Of our language and inevitably,
Cultural decadence.

"In the Millennium, everyone will be world-notorious for fifteen
minutes."

First Gray Hair

"Nowadays a women's first gray hair—is her last."
Once a widespread maxim, but one accepted too fast.
Aging continues, gray hair under the dye progressing,
Like a canary in a mine, indicates things are regressing.

The first gray hair is an indication of the direction,
That the body takes and continues at conception.
Fertilized ova, at a known rate, deteriorate.
So fewer than ninety percent of them propagate.

Gray hair usually the first indication of aging,
That the body continually new problems is staging.
Grubbing out weeds in an overgrazed pasture,
Will not halt the ensuing ecological disaster.

Gray hair tends the creases and lines to soften,
Resulting from worshipping the sun too often.
To minimize the ravages of time is fine,
Classical make-up and style work sublime.

A true blonde in her forties is pretty rare,
Except Scandinavians with naturally fair hair.
Hair dyed dark or bleached severely,
Hides nothing and enhances rarely.

Genome

A recent lay article states,
"The human genome has three billion letters."
What comes to mind is, "What kind of letters?
Arabic, Roman, Cyrillic, Hieroglyphics, Chinese symbols?"

The fact is there aren't any "letters" in our genome.
Scientists have assigned letters to chemical entities,
Shorthand for describing the make-up of genetic material,
Permitting the scientists to communicate more effectively.

A tremendous task is underway to define the human genome,
In which there are 3 billion of these chemicals.
When complete, these data can be used to prevent or treat,
The 5,000 genetic diseases in the human population.

The human genome holds hereditary characteristics,
A specific combination for each and every person.
Already DNA testing is used for forensic purposes,
Genetic profiles will join fingerprints in standard records.

Grades

She bought a bra, went to check-out,
Embarrassed to have a cup sized "A."
Cost, with tax, $31.26, tendered two twenties.
Bills bundled, change on top, half land on floor.

"Count the change to a dollar,
Then count dollars to amount tendered."
Instructions to clerks absent or ignored.
Simple operation, seldom done; store graded an "F."

But breast with cup size "A" is graded an "A,"
By men with good love-making technique.
Often desire an "A" for obvious reason,
Able to circle completely with lips.

A problem arises that with much caressing,
The "A" becomes a "B," even higher.
But that doesn't happen overnight.
Better to start at "A" rather than "C" or "D."

Heating Up

She wouldn't say yes, she wouldn't say no,
So I continued on apace.
Should I stop now, or press on?
Guess I'll do just that.
What choice do I have anyway?
Have I gone too far?
Decisions, decisions.
Guess I'll just keep pushing.
Now the moment of truth.
It's hard to please her,
"Damn. Once again the chili's too hot."

Lifetime Trauma

You can sympathize with others' disaster traumas,
But how much if you've not experienced such dramas?
The post-incident pain is with them forever,
Unable to extricate, no matter how clever.

Hurricanes, tornadoes, tsunamis, forest fires,
Earthquakes, mud-slides, floods, other undesires,
Are examples of natural phenomena's wrath.
Any one will devastate if you're in its path.

The violence of humans can devastate,
Those who hate women show rage in rape,
Some people kill, burglarize, plunder, steal.
Deja vu of horror, victims repeatedly feel.

We had boated to Bimini, on vacation for a week.
Back in Fort Lauderdale, it was rest we did seek.
It was eight o'clock, we had a light snack,
Showered quickly and then hit the sack.

In a deep sleep, at eleven-thirty waking,
With the sound of something noisily breaking.
By the night-light in the kitchen saw a figure,
By his flashlight's glow, he looked big, then bigger.

From a hearty, "Hey," he went on his way,
But would that work another day?
We had no bat, no gun on the shelf,
What could we have done to protect ourself?

Luckily the intruder, who two dead-bolts had shattered,
Was long gone. To us more disturbing things mattered.
Why us? Where we hit at random, just a pawn,
Or was it UPS stickers on the door, the uncut lawn?

"He came by water," the Policeman said,
He praised the Caniner, patted his head.
"Obviously unusual, since he came by boat.
There aren't too many crooks afloat."

"You have to protect yourselves," he said,
"We haven't the wherewithal to protect every head."
So despite an aversion to guns in the house,
We have a 357 Magnum to blast any louse.

The victims of any disaster, never fully recover,
The simple, usual things make you remember.
If the dog hits the dresser in the middle of the night,
We're immediately alert, awake with a fright.

We're empathetic to all who through trauma are stressed,
Our thoughts are with the victims, even though blessed
With the prayers and kind thoughts of myriads,
They will always have recurring, frightening periods.

Love

Love.

Do you just have to
wait?

Love can't be
forced.

When it comes you will
know.

If you settle for
less,

You will not be
transformed.

But love changes
everything.

Moving On West

Nineteenth Century—the old way of moving West:

The lure of unlimited free land,
The thrill of a new beginning,
Drove many people to sell out,
Load up the Conestoga and "Head West."

Not all Conestogas survived the rugged,
Deep ruts of the Oregon or Santa Fe trails.
If the wagon, or the oxen, broke down,
The Homesteaders staked a plot in that locale.

Twenty-first Century—the modern way of moving West:

Cut by a firm that's downsizing, whatever,
The adventurous ones relocate, head West,
To Minneapolis, Kansas City, finally Santa Fe.
Companies foot the bill, moving tired furniture.

End of the line, disillusioned, retirement looms.
Costs thousands to move to desired goal.
Invest own money relocating? Never.
Do they like it, fit in? No choice. They're marooned.

Mylan

"At seven, my son liked to play dolls,
Had pictures of fairies on his bedroom walls.
Never would I want to have any other,
Than a son who truly adores his Mother.

"At ten, I tried to keep him pure,
But now this problem to endure.
But boys at this age experiment,
Don't do things with evil intent.

"At fifteen, maybe I was too lax,
But now I have to face the facts,
My son, to girls has an aversion.
Perhaps summer boys' camp for a diversion.

"At eighteen, away from home.
I'm sure he must feel all alone.
But the Services, with aggressive boys,
Can lead a son to carnal joys.

"Now comes the reverse of all I believed.
Of active duty he's been relieved.
I kept him too close, I'm to blame,
Now we both must bear the shame.

"But newer research shows I'm free.
The fault isn't only borne by me.
Genes and peers have the major impacts,
I'm emancipated, embracing the new facts."

Perception

In England, stealing a sheep was a capitol crime.
"May as well be hung for a sheep as a lamb, they said.
Can this be extrapolated, ridiculous or sublime,
To equate sexual acts with those in the head?

Perception is reality, changes dramatically.
So that today, holding one's hand,
Is considered a form of adultery,
An accepted maxim, throughout the land.

Normal psychologists opine, when attractive women met,
Are viewed in a sexual, seed-scattering way,
It's accepted for males to look, try to get.
Thus committing adultery every day.

Lust in the heart once considered the same,
As today when your hand in another you place.
It is logical, in any case there is blame,
To go the "full course" the music to face.

Poet Confined

The case load had been heavy, her demeanor grave,
The Pueblo Style house, far from town on a hill.
The psychologist wearily opens the door.
The poet slumped sleeping over the desk.
Crumpled sheets litter the floor.
"Good thing I know he doesn't drink,
Wonder what wore him out?"
Sheets in the printer tell the tale:

The virgin ice gleams diamond white,
Fairy ghosts exit flakes of snow.
Esthetic neurons flashing bright,
Flood the whole brain a rosy glow.

Should we relax, go with the flow?
Or struggle onward to the peak?
Fighting always from below,
The top pinnacle we must seek.

They say the heart is not the source,
Of endless love, devotion, selection.
That the brain rules, but, of course,
Those who've never fallen, lack affection.

A deep sigh. "Guess I can't give up my day job."

Politically Correct

To follow the party line in Russia,
Other Communist countries, Politically Correct.
People had to spout "truths,"
Although they didn't believe them.

So now when Communism has changed,
Isn't so pervasive,
Why are we not allowed to tell,
What we see and perceive?

Truth is a myth,
Never an absolute,
Fads, misconceptions, preconceptions,
That at the moment we must embrace.

Vociferous minorities,
Backed by Liberals,
Have turned our accepted truths,
Upside down and backwards.

Poisson distribution,
Applies to all endeavors.
Half have an IQ below 100.
Dumbing down education works the same.

The average college grad today,
Equal to high school grads,
Forty years ago.
About 5 percent have college knowledge.

But you can't say that,
And you can't report what you see,
Only follow the line, be Politically Correct,
On myriads of other issues.

Psyche Enhanced

Carolyn, celebrity's breath snuffed out,
One wonders what life is all about.
Once again a soul splits, each part
Transmitted to those with fullness of heart.
So you can expect another transfusion.
More power to you, out of confusion.

Pygmalion Marriages

Marriages often have a Pygmalion relationship,
More frequently than is evident to others.
The mentor aware the other wishes to change,
The desires of the protege not fully romantic.

The motivations are a desire to learn and to teach.
One spouse is in a different kind of class,
The intention of the other to move up in some area
Or to be transported into another realm.

These often turn out to be desirable matings.
For which there are very good reasons,
Both are fulfilled in their egotistical desires,
Affection following mutual fulfillment.

Unions based on romantic love do not last,
Unless something more substantial follows.
A wedding isn't a marriage, doesn't make a marriage,
It is a reference point from which to grow.

Regrets?

Do you regret more the things you did,
Or those you didn't do?
Do you dwell more on "did" or "didn't?"

Do you remember an opportunity to help,
To give a lift, monetary, spiritual, physical?
Did you or did you not seize the moment?

Do you ponder the results of a major decision,
In your work, life or love?
Has that helped in deciding on other occasions?

Do you wonder about people who have ignored you,
Taken an instant dislike to you?
Do you think it's you or no fault of yours?

Do you often consider should I have bought something,
A major purchase, some form of ticket, some item?
Are you more concerned when you didn't buy?

If you've thought deeply about these,
Not sorrowfully, but on the road to making happier choices,
Then you'll sharpen your decisions, live a balanced life.

Relative Holidays

"Five o'clock," the radio blares, "Must crawl out of bed."
So Betty sighed as she shook clear her head.
Rolled off the bed, trudged to the shower.
Thought better of it, "If I stir Ed, he'll holler.
His bellowing will wake the kids too soon,
I'd be happy if they'd sleep till noon."

Dress the turkey, trim the ham,
Bake the bread, prepare the lamb.

"My God it's nearly seven.

"I'll just get everything else in line.
Where and what do I do with the time?
It won't be long before they pile in.
Heaven forbid they'll be contributing.

"My God, it's almost eleven.

"I've got to shower, get out of these clothes.
Damn, there's the doorbell, it's Cousin Rose.
With all her tribe and her fat husband, Sam,
Bellowing, 'Where's the ham.' Hell, he's not worth Spam.

"Fifteen minutes out to dress, splash on goop,
But who's to notice in this group?
Sixteen vultures all crowding around,
Like the first meal they've ever found.

"Now the meals over, the crowds having fun,
Criticizing all the cooking I've done.
They sit and watch the slaving jerk.
No help to clean up. 'Betty likes to work.'

"By the time I'm finished it's mid-afternoon,
And they're all picking, got a different tune.
'You can't possibly eat this stuff on your own.'
They parcel it up and take it all home.

"No 'Thank You' or notes in coming weeks.
Even though it's not kudos one seeks.
But they'll be back for the next great feast.

Thanksgiving et al., they all have a word,
It's the story before every festivity heard.
'Whole cranberries, spiral sliced ham,
Don't give my husband any of that Spam.
Irish and sweet potatoes, we want to choose.
Single crust pies you can quickly lose.
Double crusts are all we can take,
And dilute down the coffee, it keeps us awake.'

"Is it worth waiting till the kids are in college?
Or time to head off to my own little cottage?
The revenge: to come back and criticize.
But would they ever realize?

"Likely they'd opt for a restaurant, everyone pays.
For a cost that at home they'd live several days,

"I've tried to be a dutiful wife,
But I'm not stuck here for the rest of my life."

Romance Novels

"He kissed her lips hard, until they bled.
She smiled expectantly, her teeth bright red."
If this is your idea of making love romantically,
And forever seeking a 'White Knight,' frantically,
Then you're likely an avid reader of romance novels,
They're a mainstay of women in mansions and hovels.

What makes women adore novels like these?
Whether written to titillate or merely to please,
Offer high hopes of fond love that ever will last,
Deep emotions and feelings unknown in the past.
What are the reasons for this cavernous affliction,
Is it because men use them, offer no real affection?

Those most interested in others' careers and lives,
Have nothing to cling to or treasure and prize.
Similarly nebulous desires swirl endlessly here.
Reading a book one can fantasize, no thoughts to fear.
Dreams surge for awhile: Mistakes never made,
Bodies virginal and pristine, while sorrows fade.

Run, Run, Run

The earth at a thousand miles per hour is spun,
Circling at sixty-six thousand 'round the sun.
And that cop for going ninety stopped me,
I was running late, couldn't he see?

I was off to day care center with Meg.
Did he expect to avoid a ticket I'd beg?
So he wrote the ticket and took his time.
I finished my mascara, To Hell with the fine.

I pulled into line while combing my hair,
Didn't know why that damn post was there.
It looks like a little scratch to me,
But Bob'll say it's costly, we won't agree.

With all that I got to work an hour late,
Had to explain why, something I hate.
Two patients had left before I arrived,
If not, to serve them I'd have contrived.

By five I'd finished off the last three.
Out of the office I had to flee,
To the market to get food for dinner,
I started to think, "Sure married a winner."

About my husband, my friends all rave,
Think nothing of the fact I'm a slave.
An ex-football player, selling cars,
Spending his time after work in bars.

An Animal Doctor, I have to keep up
With the latest treatments for a pup.
This women's liberation is not for me,
I'll take Meg and leave, then I'll be free.

Santa Fe Muse

Is it truly the climate salubrious,
In the City and County Different,
Or the fabled sunsets of rich sensation,
For which artists work for less?
Or equally the reflections of sunrise over Sangre de Cristo,
Panoramic and truly as vivid as blood?
Or is the essence the comingling of like spirits,
That face, exchange, cavort, embrace,
Until all acquire streams of creativity?
Energizing flights of fancy,
In varied and individual wavelengths,
Reverberating across time and space.

She Said

She said, "You've got great buns."
But was it only to butter me up?
She said, "I'm totally yours forever."
A double quantum leap into the unknown.

She said, "We'll be married in the millennium."
But she thought of the millennium as reincarnation.
Like the man who completely misunderstood terminology,
Told the surgeon castration, but meant circumcision.

"Does reincarnation really exist," I asked.
"We'll have to wait and see won't we," she replied.
If it truly exists, will she get our rebirths in sync?
She said, "Of course." But where's the guarantee?

Shoppers

As a man I do shopping like a surgeon,
Who, peering through a fiber optic,
Snips off a small gland or a minute tumor.

I'm cognizant of the item to buy,
With tunnel vision, laser accuracy,
I head for the department, the counter.

A woman shopping has a different approach.
Takes note of every department, every display.
If not an item for today, maybe tomorrow.

Where did these contrary moves originate?
Men went out to hunt, eyes concentrating on prey.
Women gathered, spotting future plants along the path.

While both sexes performed their survival ways,
There is no need today for men's singular focus,
Women's scrutiny still serves a worthwhile need.

Women's techniques survived the transition.
Men's methods have become anachronistic,
They need to widen their peripheral vision.

Single Mothers

For centuries religions prophesized,
That a human God, a Messiah, would appear.
It was a fantasy not taken literally,
Until Christ's birth. But what was the year?

Historians say not later than 04 BC,
According to the calendar used in this hemisphere.
Scientists using Chinese records say 04 AD.
In either case when is, or was, the Millennium here?

The end of the Twentieth Century is December 31, 2000.
The Twenty-First Century begins January 1, 2001, not before.
If we go with the historians, the Millennium is past.
The Chinese supernova report says wait four years more.

Since gender is determined by the male sperm,
Only a female would result from a parthenogenetic birth.
But the myth of this baby, born of a virgin,
Relentlessly spread, throughout the earth.

Today are we surrounded by virgin births?
All we hear about is "single mothers."
No, it's a euphemism for something else.
Unwed, deserted, separated, widows, divorcees, others.

Others, because with modern science, it's possible,
To extract from a fertilized ovum, DNA from the male,
By further manipulation to put in only DNA from the mother.
Voila, the offspring is completely from the female.

So today a single mother could bear,
Something that may seem far away,
An *in vitro* true clone of herself.
The science for this is here today.

To Joan

Shouldn't every man want an intelligent wife?
Perhaps even one of superior physique?
Does it diminish any aspect of your life?
Not at all because each of us is unique.

Companion who thinks deeply, with emotion,
Whose enlightened conclusions are ones to ponder.
It is truly great joy for healthy relations,
And smooths the way to a buoyant blue yonder.

While clear that ideal matings can take place
From arranged marriages, they are quite rare,
They come more readily when free choice operates.
They evolve from true love, to couples who care.

To have a wife superior and completely true,
Is a wonderful thing, it can happen to you.

To Kelly

Vibrant, effervescent, come immediately to mind.
Talent to spare, she helps everyone around.
Caring and concern are among things that bind.
Whatever the subject, helpful aids abound.

Skilled at ballet, all facets of the dance.
Using her intellect in business to progress.
Agility with exercise, her figure to enhance.
Ability and hard work fostering success.

As may be gleaned from the above short lines,
These assets are housed in a superior case.
Fortunate are those who share precious times,
But find it not easy to keep up her pace.

Startlingly unique, and exceedingly fun,
Blessed you will be when her favor you've won.

Spincialists

When Time Magazine in nineteen eighty-eight,
Coined the term "spin" it referred,
To politicians positioning themselves,
Very cleverly, on complex and controversial issues.

Today, spin equals lies, fabrication.
Spin doctors alter facts to suit their objective,
Which is a disregard for truth to make their point.
It is the sleazy side of public relations.

Stock brokers spin worthless stock.
Bankers spin mergers and acquisitions.
Accountants spin standard accounting rules,
To keep clients and get consulting contracts.

Pitchers spin hardballs.
Sharks spin cue balls,
Politicians spin indiscretions.
Publicists spin endlessly.

To a mathematician, $2+2 = 3.6$ to 4.5.
A scientist puts the best possible case for a theory.
A FDA submission is presented in the most positive light.
A potential suitor shows only the good side.

All of these are spins and some a needed endeavor.
Not to show uplifting things,
Even out of despair,
Would make life intolerable.

Little white lies, slanted reports,
Are normal and necessary.
But if spin is a means to grossly deceive,
Then it takes on a whole new connotation.

The New Designers

It used to be that those who designed,
Were closer to the building kind.
After specialization, University degrees,
Architects worked only for fees.
They had no construction, hands-on work,
No more physical labor than a clerk.

But now the architects begin to find,
They need experience of the craftsman kind.
So in Maine, they gather annually,
To meet with tradesmen and work manually.

For our new house, the plans were drawn,
By a carpenter, once working with brawn,
But now a contractor in the Southwest,
Building with adobe, material he likes best.

With some major inputs from us as well,
It makes a true home, great place to dwell.
A house that has a Feng Shui feeling,
Everyone who enters finds it appealing.

To A Landscape Architect Trainee

Tote that bag of seed, tamp in that plant,
Follow the plan, not possible to recant.
A mild winter and a great spring season,
If the flowers don't bloom, there must be a reason.
But it can't possibly be the planter,
Guess we'll blame it all on the mentor.

To Heal A Broken Heart

Channel blockers, alpha and beta blockers,
Angiotensin converting enzyme inhibitors,
Diuretics, anginal preparations, vasodilators,
Are all used to heal ailing hearts.

But heart medication won't heal a "broken" heart.
The problem is seated in the brain,
Not in the organ, which romantic writing,
Has given the origin of all feelings.

But that doesn't mean that our hearts.
Aren't affected, don't feel heavy,
Don't have hypertension, or fibrillation,
Perhaps feel like they'll burst.

We're told the depression will pass,
That Time will heal the pain,
A tranquilizer will help.
Maybe so, but maybe not.

For some the heart recovers quickly,
Others find it not so glib.
Some minds commit for eternity,
Others shrug, start a new pursuit.

To The Writer In You

She wrote obscurely, but with nothing to hide,
They said, "It's too deep to ever survive."
She tried to write clearly, at a New York pace,
They said, "We hate that stuff in our face."

Both approaches were wrong, following popular ways.
Change my style, she thought, to what sells these days?
Can one be a chameleon, change that fast?
If you do will acclaim persist, fame last?

Finally it all depends on desire,
To write commercially or because you're on fire.
Is being able, essay or poem to sell,
The criterion by which you'll be known quite well?

If you haven't a pure and lasting compulsion,
Will you end up with a deep revulsion?
Writing to satisfy what others may rate,
Completing your efforts with output you hate?

Strive for confidence not to write sleaze,
Nor to follow fashion, the public to please.
Is the editor's view better or worse?
The view of bad critics becomes a true curse.

Think through, assess the talents at hand,
No matter they're not tops in the land.
Don't worry because you can't sing, draw or play.
Work the skills that you have, every way, every day.

With reasonable ability, hard work and persistence,
You'll reach your goals, allay all resistance.

What Are Yours?

Have you ever stopped running long enough,
To consider what is important to you?
To state the two areas you follow the most.
To yourself, at least, you should be true.

With some it's greed, hoarding, wealth,
Combined with a workaholic life.
Often entwined with then acquiring,
A young, slim, blonde, trophy wife.

Have you been devoting your life to your kids?
Not been accepting the facts of life?
Genes and peers matter, nurturing minor?
Better by far be good husband or wife.

Maybe it's living vicariously,
Championing a sports team avidly.
Add chasing fun, avoiding all pain,
The sum approaches real depravity.

One or more of the arts,
You could relentlessly pursue,
Plus, perhaps, environmentalist fervor,
In the areas of most concern to you.

Power to control is a vicious vice,
At work, with family or at play.
If this occurs with control of money,
It propagates misery every day.

What can you do to find your way?
Isn't it not worth living, the unexplored life?
Think through what you need, where you want to go,
Approach each day boldly but with minimum strife.

What It Takes

First of all it takes a vision, an idea.
It may be a completely new concept,
More likely to be incremental.

Some talent in the area chosen is essential.
With a major ability less moil is required.
But super effort plus minor ability equals success.

Perseverance is a dominant prerequisite.
Remember the classical tale of the miner,
Who stopped ten feet from a major vein of gold.

Finally, it takes marketing skills,
To assess the projected or suggested need,
Then to figure a "must have" pitch.

You're never a failure until you quit.

Wishes

I wish you work that is fulfilling,
Giving your best, able and willing.

I wish you time to relax, to play,
A pleasant fun time in every day.

I wish you agility and health,
A major part of total wealth.

I wish you joy and happiness galore,
So you couldn't want for anything more.

I wish you love, to get, to give,
The main reason for one to live.

I wish you relaxing, rewarding vacations,
Sunning, cruising, hiking, uplifting elations.

I wish you may fulfill any good scheme,
No matter if on the far side it may seem.

I wish that every strong dream you envision,
Will come to pass, with only minor revision.

MISCELLANEOUS

A Chinese Puzzle

Anything peculiar, strange, exotic or esoteric,
Is in the vernacular, "Chinese."
Pomegranates are peculiar, so they're "Chinese apples."
People running around randomly are a "Chinese fire drill."

Grandson Edmund has a Fire Chief Halloween costume,
One made in China to boot, although that's not evident.
But if it were known what would people conclude?
Would they think this kid was running around in circles?

The strange thing is that the Chinese were
The most advanced of civilizations,
Centuries ahead of the Western World,
And were probably the first to have communities.

Marco Polo brought back fireworks and pasta.
But we attribute the latter delicacy to Italians.
Is it because the Chinese have the gene for slant eyes?
Or maybe the color of their skin?

Perhaps a combination of factors is operative.
Language and writing not understood,
They look different. Physique unique?
People believe the weirdest things.

Best Sellers

What books are consistently best sellers?
According to some local literary gurus,
Bibles and books featuring recipes or animals.
All three categories are constantly in demand

Bibles

People fear the unknown. Some ten thousand years ago,
Egyptians and Orientals studied the bodies in the Heavens,
Spotted Orion, a major constellation, and concluded,
That was where they would go when they died.

Religions are based on fear, superstition, and ritual.
The founders of religions had to consider all three.
The priests, sages or whomever, addressed some of these
By manuscripts, called Bibles, Korans, or whatever.

These documents, written by man, were attributed,
To some Higher Power residing in outer space.
In the Judeo-Christian Bibles, choices had to be made
As to which writings would best allay fear and superstition.

Over several millennia the Jewish Bible was standardized,
Leaders of the Christian religion, from numerous sources,
Chose what is known today as The New Testament,
But they excluded many reports of miraculous cures.

Having cared for the immediate needs of congregations,
Fear and superstition still being present,
But somewhat explained, panic was subdued,
Then they developed rituals, to keep members adhering.

Recipes

Food is essential to life and in advanced societies,
It is not just eating rice or corn, or some other staple,
But the social intercourse of meals, and, of course,
The plus of esthetic appearance and intriguing taste.

As well as the American approach to fast food,
All ethnic groups have added to the repertoire.
Regional recipes, once served in sheltered areas,
Are now served routinely across the land.

Today we have a Universal sharing of different cuisines.
The French have had marked influence for a long time,
Japanese cooking and ingredients have had a major run,
Sushi being very popular. Thai dishes are nationwide.

California has spread the use of salads, fresh vegetables.
Vegetarian diets, of varying kinds, have multiplied.
Foods grown without chemicals, or gene manipulation,
So called, "organic foods," are expensive but popular.

Recipe books, based on new or modified approaches
Or combined with diet regimens, emerge daily.
Sometimes the book is targeted for a specific use,
As, for example, quick recipes for boaters or RV travelers.

Animals

We are so closely tied to our pet and companion animals,
That they are an integral part of our lives and literature.
Not only do they show us by their actions,
What we have lost, but they teach us ways to grow.

Animals help humans in various and essential ways.
Beasts of burden go where vehicles cannot.
Animal products and services ensure our health.
Zoo animals educate, while preserving endangered species.

Who doesn't know of the healing power of animals?
Riding horses gives confidence to handicapped children,
Seniors petting animals gives them succor,
And lowers their blood pressure significantly.

Dogs pull sleds over the frozen tundra,
Seeing-eye dogs give mobility to the blind.
Others help the wheelchair bound to live alone.
Herding and hunting dogs serve useful purposes.

Homo sapiens, designated a higher species,
Over eons has evolved from a common ancestor,
Even though it is a extremely difficult leap,
For many humans to consider or to admit.

Man does not live on Earth in isolation,
Were it not for the complex ecology,
With sun, water, plants, animals and minerals,
Humans could not continue to exist.

Continental Drift

Those who ignore geography,
Are bound to mess things up.
Or maybe just, by coincidence, simplify.

The term African-American implies.
That all Africa is one country,
And populated only by blacks.
Aren't Egyptians, Algerians et al.
Also African-Americans?

Black slaves in general came from Africa's West Coast,
Mainly sold by their enslaving peers.
But still there were countries, separate regions.

There are no "Native Americans,"
Some sixty-five million years ago,
The last of the dinosaurs roamed the Americas.
Man appeared on Earth a couple million years ago.

Ten thousand years ago, Polynesians migrated to California.
Second came Europeans, and finally,
The American Indians crossing the land bridge from Asia.
The first and third groups were from Asia.

The "continental" designation carried to the extreme
Results in only four categories of hyphenated U.S. citizens:
African-Americans, Asian-Americans,
Australian-Americans, European-Americans.

No more Irish Americans, German Americans,
Polish Americans, English Americans.
The Israelis and Arabs are now Asian Americans.
Countries have gone by the boards.

Daily Life

Every day choices are made.
Don't look back and don't be afraid.
That is, don't look back in order to weep,
But retrospective thinking may help a heap.

Plan for the future, that's where life lies,
Use every moment, it's true "time flies."
Remember always to stick to the path,
The Diamond Back in the weeds, shares his wrath.

You should stop to smell the roses,
Regulate the time that work imposes.
Have some fun, play games too,
And to yourself strive to be true.

Decimation

When you ponder the destruction in the Southwest,
Where human population pressures have never been extreme,
It is disturbing to imagine the worldwide devastation,
Which will result from today's six billion humans.

Open pit and strip mining scar the Nation.
Why were we so late in legislating restoration?
Pollution of lakes, rivers, the oceans continues,
Deforestation relentlessly lowers our water tables.

In Northern New Mexico, once covered with grass,
There is now bare earth between Juniper trees.
The downgrading continues at an accelerated pace,
As UV light and heat keep bacteria from their mission.

Knowledge slowly trickles down to the producer,
Even when solutions are known, economics rule.
Soil conservation if practiced the last hundred years,
Would have preserved the pastures for future generations.

Criticism of Government, especially EPA, is subsiding.
Progress is being made in educating our youth.
Most people now deplore environmental neglect.
Ignoring ecological disasters is now unacceptable.

Enchanted (In the Land of Enchantment)

I didn't think it possible,
Thought it implausible,
That with the first locking of eyes,
I'd experience my greatest surprise.

It was like a supernova, so bright,
My eyes blinked at the fiery light.
In previous incarnation we were one,
So instantly my heart you won.

At once we were bound forever,
With a cord so neat and clever,
An invisible bond of whatever medium,
Which can stretch from zero to continuum.

Our birthdates aren't the best connection,
But our thoughts flew in the right direction,
To meet at a mutually agreeable place,
Our minds bridging time and space.

I didn't think it possible,
Might have considered it laughable.
But the enchantment overwhelmed my heart,
Instantly I knew we'd never part.

Flat Tire Nineteenth Century

As the Conestogas headed West,
Wooden wheels, dried out, shrank.
The iron rims didn't shrink,
Were loose, could drop off.

If the rim were observed
Before it fell off,
The wheel could be saved,
The rim resized, refitted.

One area of rim heated to cherry red,
A section cut out, diameter then too small.
A rim of fire around the rim, causes expansion.
When hot too big on wheel, when cool fit snugly.

Not all rims and wheels held up.
Oregon and Santa Fe deep ruts, took their toll.
If the wagon, oxen or people reached their limit,
A homestead was staked in that locale.

June Enchantment

The sky over the Mesa is startlingly blue.
Intricate ice-crystal patterns in wispy cirrus clouds.
Cumulonimbus clouds kiss the Sangre de Cristo range,
"Old Baldy" still wearing a snow cap.

Commercial jet trails crisscross the troposphere,
Making a familiar template for tic-tac-toe.
Air Force fighters fill in the spaces for X's and O's.
A ballet at sonic and subsonic speeds.

One day in May there were nine Bluebirds on the spa,
Gone north, their feeder with suet and sunflower seeds idle,
The House Finches have different tastes,
Struggling to feed their newborn under our eaves.

In the high desert, xeriscape plants have an edge.
The spring battle between grasses and weeds in full swing.
Tumbleweed roots descend deep below the shallow top soil.
Blue grama, planted a year ago, tentatively pokes up.

Metaphors

When writing contemporary poetry,
The way to write with the "in" crowd,
As defined by the reigning poets,
Is to use metaphors. Lots of them.

"Our Irish Wolfhound's moves are studied intensely.
Her odoriferous farts produce emesis in *Homo sapiens,*
Farts emerge like heat waves from the African continent,
Which spawn killer hurricanes in North America."

Why are obscure comparisons believed to be,
More acceptable than telling it clearly?
Is it because one can think fuzzily,
When comparing an action with something else?

Millennium

Christ's birth from 4 B.C. to 4 A.D. is dated,
Whether an historian or astronomer has rated.
The date of the Millennium is really not known,
So pull up the screen and figure your own.

The Millennium really begins on January 1, 2001.
But popular belief, means people have Y2K fun
Toasting New Year's 2000. But never fear,
We celebrated commercially for a whole year.

Since the Second Century A.D.,in rhyme,
The Millennium was considered a mystical time.
Today it is not a huge stretch to face,
January 2001, new Millennium, reincarnation embrace.

Names

My name is "Maplesden."
A thousand-year-old English name,
Coined in Kent County.
Maple trees, creating a copse or den.

Have you three or more syllables in your name?
If so you are in for endless pain.
Especially in an Hispanic area,
If your name, as mine, has a hard "A."

Maplesden is fairly straight forward,
"Maples" as in "trees' and "den" as in "lion's den."
The Hispanics want to start with "map,"
A soft "A" as in pap.

But wait.
The Hispanics aren't as bad,
As the Anglos in fouling up.
I've been addressed as "Napoleon,"
Introduced as "Finkelstein."

Had the following:
"Doctor Maplestein?"
"No, it's Maplesden."
"Oh, Doctor Maplesdenstein."

I've been "Douglas Maplesdeno,"
And every other variation you might imagine.
Mapleston, Maplestone, Maplesdon, M. Aplesden, et al.

Even two-syllable names are not exempt,
As I've been addressed as "Donglas,"
Duggy, Duggle, Dougie, Dugglass, Dugless.
Any wonder I write under the pen name, D.C.Maples?

When I'm at the Pearly Gates,
And St. Peter reads from the Holy Roster,
"No such name as yours for this date,
Banned to Purgatory, we'll call you."

Parallel Worlds

You hear a lot about "multiple personalities."
Then you read that most of them are hoaxes.
Ponder a moment, don't most of us have more than one?

There is the real world with which we cope daily,
Where some may act out a studied persona.
How honest is our presentation?

Simultaneously there is a dream world,
And that can be sleeping,
Or day-dreaming while awake.

So there are:

Parallel Worlds

Fantacies while awake are concocted.
Can dreams be controlled?
If so, would you choose to "dream up" nightmares?

If you make an effort, plan to remember night dreams,
Chances are you can, but then can't filter out scary ones.
Whether or not you dream in color appears to be genetical,

What is evident is there are:

Parallel Worlds

Soluna Worship

The sun and the moon have been the object
For worship of many cultures.
Their cycles are not difficult to record, to plot.
They are tangible, easy to teach.
They do not require a leap of faith,
Their visible courses are proven.
They do not force one to endure
Pain, unbearable conditions,
In the hope of an afterlife.

Thus to celebrate the solstices and the equinoxes,
Is to appreciate the basis of our existence.
The course of the moon
Daily affects the oceans' tides.
At its distance from Earth,
Keeps the wobble at an acceptable level.
Without the moon and sun
 There could be no life as we know it.

The planets, with their courses more difficult
To understand, to plot, to teach
Have not the simple appeal of the sun and moon.
At present do not have a major influence
On today's life on Earth

Worship based on the sun and moon,
Is not subjected to debate and change by humans.
It is a constant and does not have
Fear, superstition and ritual
As do other religions.

Sounds

Morning gray slowly gives way
To the scarlet laser ray
Of the sun squinting over
Glorieta Mesa,
Painting red corpuscles
On the clouds over the
Sangre de Cristo mountains.

Here in this bucolic area,
The nearest neighbor north,
More than a quarter mile,
Where one expects to experience
The quiet life,
The cacophony is overwhelming.
Even to insensitive ears.

The 4X4, delivering the New Mexican,
Changes gears, lines up with the box,
Emitting a backing-up beep, beep warning.
The coyotes fling their last night howl.
The crows begin a persistent caw, caw,
The house finches filling in silent spaces,
With their higher pitched cheep, cheep.

The Doppler whooee, whooee of a freight train,
Entering the Glorieta Pass, gives way
To a tighter whoo, whoo as it comes abeam,
Maintains that sound to Lamy and then
As it moves toward Galisteo,
Reverts to the Doppler effect of,
More whooee's, until the whistle fades.

The Irish Wolfhound on her bed,
Gives several ear rattling moumoueees,
Her version of a waking yawn.
While not to be outdone,
The twenty pound, pushy, alley cat,
Scratches at the bedroom door,
While emitting soprano myrrrowes.

A helicopter whirrs overhead,
While at higher altitudes,
The jet planes heading north or south.
At troposphere heights, whine their paths,
Above the noisier, slower commuter planes
Changing the pitch of their propellers
As they descend to Santa Fe airport.

An anemic hum of traffic, a mile distant on U.S. 285.
High wind pushing vainly on adobe walls,
But roaring down the living room fireplace,
Whistling down the pipes to the great room stove.
Neighing of horses on nearby ranches,
Interspersed with barking of ranch dogs.
Soughing of pine trees swaying in the wind.

No alarm clock to shatter pleasant dreams,
But responsibilities and subconscious solutions
To business problems, break the surface to awake
Long before the piercing ring of a clock,
Or the blare of grating talk radio,
Now superseded by the Today Show.
Beating one or more old stories to a frazzle.

The water pipes clang, clang, clang,
From excessive air in the water,
A legacy of the engineering genius
Of the Local Utilities Company.
This also makes a sputter, sputter
As the toilet is flushed, and reprised
When showers continue the ablutions.

The normal sounds of a modern kitchen.
The gentle hum of compressors cooling,
Or freezing, food in the refrigerators.
The dishwasher squirting water to cleanse
Dishes, flatware, glasses, pots and pans.
Boiling kettle whistling an urgent message.
Ice cubes crunching into an empty tray.

Overarching all of this the soft murmur
Of computers, spinning their hard disks,
With urgent messages from the speakers.
The click, click, click of the keyboards.
But no car horns, engine or jake brake grinds,
No police, sheriff, ambulance or fire sirens.
The sun is now warming the inviting portale.

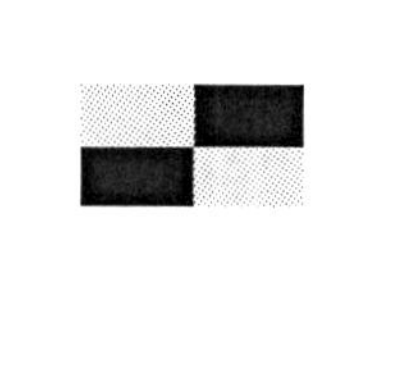

Suddenly Snow

"Snow will fall at eight thousand feet high."
A thousand feet higher than where we lie.
Horizontally the snowflakes blow,
Bringing us wet and clinging snow.

Not the snow of the dry desert high,
But the kind you see when ocean is nigh.
Juniper and pinon, so sparkling, seem
To have been coated with diamond-laced cream.

In the north, Sangre de Cristo, eminence gray,
Old Baldy's pate a platinum toupee.
In the west, the Jemez shine stark white.
East, Glorieta Mesa glowing bright.

Southwest, majestic Monzanos loom tall,
The Sandias behind, dominate all.
Both snow-capped crests, a pretty sight.
New ski season starting just right.

On the portale, snow-covered fireplace wood,
Reminding of work not done but should.
Summer furniture to the garage to pack,
Courtyard chaise longues inside to stack.

Four inches of the white stuff, won't last,
Has disappeared quickly in the past.
Rumored in two days it evaporates,
But here it likely sublimates.

Over the stoop the new roof hovers,
Ice no longer the concrete covers.
Grama grass in the bitter wind blows,
Proudly it faces all future snows.

Index of Titles

Printed in the United States
200424BV00005B/172-180/A